REIGATE & REDHILL
PAST & PRESENT

Mount Walk, Earlswood, *c.* 1910.

London Road, *c.* 1904. The caption on this postcard describes the scene as 'old & new Reigate' although there is not yet much sign of the 'new'. Change did come, but not until 1932 when the houses on the right were swept away in another road-widening scheme. King Car was making its presence felt upon the town.

Many readers who knew the town in the 1960s will remember the sweet shop called The Cigarette and Chocolate Box that stood for many years opposite the bus stop (always known then as The Red Cross bus stop) and was the first port of call for children coming into the town to visit the swimming baths.

Entrance to the Castle Grounds, London Road, *c.* 1908. The grounds, paid for by local residents, were laid out in 1873 and leased to the Borough Council by Mr Somers Somerset. In 1921 the Council bought the freehold and the five-acre site was then opened to the public.

The pretty gates have gone, replaced by an ugly metal barrier, but the grounds are still a joy to wander through when the constant drone of road traffic becomes too much.

Tunnel Road, looking east, *c.* 1910. The tunnel proved to be a popular route through the town and very nearly became a victim of its own success, as Wilfrid Hooper describes in 1945: '. . . Suggestions have also been made for demolishing the Old Town Hall and widening Tunnel Road which, if followed, will rob the town of two of its most characteristic features and hasten the process of uglification and suburbanisation.'

Tunnel Road is still much in use today by pedestrians and cyclists, and occasionally the tunnel itself is used for street markets.

Tunnel Road *c*. 1910. Made under the directions of Lord Somers through the Castle rock in 1823, it provided a direct link between Market Place and London Road. The scheme was condemned by the writer William Cobbett as wasteful, undertaken only to attract more coaching traffic. At a gate on the town side, tolls were levied: 6*d* for coach and four, 1½*d* for single horse and chaise, ½*d* for a horse, foot passengers free of charge. The Tunnel Vaults on the left were once used by the Reigate brewers Mellersh & Neale, and their entry for 1892 of *The Illustrated Business Guide to Reigate, Redhill and Horley* proudly boasts 'The proprietors also possess very extensive cellars, especially one in the Tunnel Road excavated from the sand rock and being capable of holding in store many thousands of barrels of ale. This valuable store gives the firm a great advantage over many breweries by their being able to go largely into stock, and so mature and get their ales into good condition before sending them out to customers.'

This view is virtually unchanged in 1998. Although the tunnel has not been accessible to traffic for many years, it is still a popular route for pedestrians and cyclists.

London Road. *c.* 1950. This small area of the town was a bustling little community then. The row of shops on the right, called The Broadway, clustered around the showroom and workshops of Wray Park Garages Ltd, and included the old-established portrait photographers Windsor-Spice and The Broadway Restaurant. Further along the road were four coal merchants, based at the railway sidings, namely Hall & Co., the South Suburban Co-Operative Society, Sargant & Martin, and Rickett, Cockerell & Co. Alongside these were fishmongers Lake & Humphrey, Miss Hotson's teashop and W. Kemp & Son, corn & seed merchants. Reigate bookseller Sean Hawkins recalls Miss Hotson vividly: 'One could buy some rather dubious sweets displayed in glass bottles in the front window . . . the licorice was stale and inedible, also she was quite famous for the strength of her brew, and when milk was added the colour turned to a shade in between the dark brown of her hat and that of her tawny overcoat. This overcoat was only removed on the hottest of summer days, but the hat stayed firmly in place, always.'

Many changes have taken place in the last forty years, the largest of which is the construction of huge offices for accounting company Watsons on the site of Wray Park Garage and the Swimming Baths. The whole station area is being rebuilt and a modern office has replaced The Railway Hotel.

London Road, *c.* 1940. After the Second World War many large houses were never again used as family homes and were either demolished or converted into business premises; here, the house on the left became E.J. Baker's commercial vehicle repair garage. The smaller properties on the right were, in part, owned by the railway and rented out to small businesses.

Modern office buildings now dominate the area chiefly because of the easy access to the M25 motorway at the top of Reigate Hill. The large building near the railway was built on the site of the birthplace of prima ballerina Dame Margot Fonteyn.

Reigate station, *c.* 1909. In 1849 the Reading, Guildford and Reigate Railway opened its line for business but this east–west route was not as popular as the north–south route through Redhill which connected directly to London; as Wilfrid Hooper writes, 'The east end of the parish thus sprang into prominence as a centre of railway traffic within easy reach of London, while Reigate, which had shown some hostility to the new developments, has to be content with a subordinate station on a branch line with a level-crossing obstructing the main London Road.'

The level-crossing gates have long since given way to automatic barriers and in 1997 something was finally done to rectify the terrible condition of the station buildings . . . they were demolished. A new station/office development is currently under construction (1998). The smart, quiet diesel-engined locomotives are run by Thames Trains.

Reigate station, *c*. 1910. In 1849 the Reading, Guildford and Reigate Railway had opened its line, creating a new station building where the line crossed the London Road. Until this time the station at Redhill had been called Reigate Junction, because Reigate was by far the more important town. However, this was to change as railways grew more important and the new Warwick Town grew up, to be absorbed into the thriving town of Redhill, and Reigate, offering no direct route to London, became a sub-station.

Since railway privatisation many of the newly formed operating companies have found improving services a difficult process, and many stations became severely dilapidated. The buildings at Reigate were in deplorable condition; in 1997 the old station building and the small shops on London Road were demolished to make way for a new combined office block and station building. Work started in 1998 and rail users look forward to having a station that befits its elegant town.

London Road, *c.* 1912. 'To the north, between the Railway and the Chalk Hills, are the white new villas of Wray Park,' said R.F.D. Palgrave in 1860, describing the area shown here. Once called London Lane, its name is thought to derive not from the direction in which it led, but rather from the fact that Roger de London acquired the manor of Colley in the thirteenth century.

Until very recently both sides of London Road were lined with substantial Victorian and Edwardian houses; practically all of these have been demolished to make way for many apartment blocks and smaller houses. The Reigate Register Office is a fine example of the earlier style of 'white new villa'.

The Toll-House at Reigate Hill, *c.* 1905. In 1864 Reigate Borough Council took over repair of the road between Reigate Hill and Cockshott Hill from the Reigate Trust whose responsibility it had been since the turnpike legislation of 1755. Under this Act the Trust had been able to erect turnpikes and levy tolls on traffic using the road under their charge. Most such roads were in bad condition at this period, and the state of things at Redhill roused strong protest. The scarring on the hillside attests to extensive extraction of Reigate stone, historically famous for its use since the Middle Ages in church and ornamental building work. Examples include Westminster Abbey and Palace, Windsor Castle, Hampton and Nonsuch Palaces; many less grand houses have used hearthstone mined here to scour their hearths and front steps.

The scarred hillside is now masked by trees and undergrowth and crowned by radio, television and telephone transmitter aerials.

The Yew Tree Inn, Reigate Hill, *c.* 1910. Two pubs faced each other on the approach to Reigate Hill. The Yew Tree Inn, built in 1841 and run by J. Green, was demolished in a road-widening scheme in 1938. Opposite stood The Rifle Volunteer, probably named after the formation in 1860 of the Reigate Volunteer Rifles, which later became A Company of the 2nd Volunteer Battalion of The Queen's Royal West Surrey Regiment.

The Yew Tree Inn stands at right angles to its predecessor, and a new petrol station has been built on the other side of Beech Road. The Rifle Volunteer is now a private residence.

Reigate Hill, *c.* 1910. Lodge house to The Rock, a large estate on the edge of Reigate Hill which appears on a census of 1834 as belonging to Francis Giles. By 1855 William Hackblock, leather merchant, was recorded as being the occupant along with three servants. He later served as an MP for the borough but his death in 1858 meant that his tenure of the position was the shortest. Thomas Hill JP lived at The Rock for five years until 1888 when the auction catalogue of the property describes it thus: 'The estate possesses a very long frontage to the main London Road and the approach to the house is by two carriage drives, one having a picturesque Lodge entrance covered with rose trees and creepers.'

The pretty gateway by the Lodge House has been demolished and the fine chimneys have been truncated. The Rock is now divided into four apartments.

Reigate Hill, *c.* 1930. This rather drab building was once The Black Horse public house but latterly it became Crossways Guest House. It was demolished sometime in the 1950s.

The motorway construction makes locating the old site difficult as the road has been re-aligned.

Reigate Hill, *c.* 1930. The popular Tea House at the top of Reigate Hill had been serving refreshments to travellers since 1900; unfortunately the building was completely destroyed by a doodlebug in 1944, killing the owner Mr Carey.

Since the construction of the motorway the road alignment in this area has altered slightly, but the site of the Tea House is generally acknowledged to be opposite Margery Lane.

CHAPTER TWO

REIGATE: HIGH STREET

High Street, c. 1900. This western end of the High Street had some of the town's most ancient buildings, including the old Market House and a chapel dedicated to the Holy Cross which stood near to the Red Cross Inn. In earlier times the principal entrance to the town was by Nutley Lane and there the market granted by Edward II in 1313, was held for more than 500 years. The old Market House was demolished in 1728, the same year that the Town Hall was erected. 'In 1860 a cave behind the Red Cross Inn fell in causing the partial collapse of 5 cottages erected above it, though all the occupants escaped with their lives.' (Illustrated London News, 19 May 1860.) The building on the left was the coachbuilding shop of George Burtenshaw & Sons; at one time it was the post office, run by John Skinner who became postmaster at Betchworth in 1900.

The identical scene in 1905, showing the first phase of the road-widening works that were to demolish some of Reigate's precious early buildings.

Now those pretty tile-hung buildings at the end of West Street have gone, along with those at the end of Slipshoe Street. The Red Cross Inn remains although it has become a victim of the current fashion to give pubs 'themed' names; it now sports the title of Tap & Spile.

High Street, *c*. 1890. The water pump in the centre of the road was removed by the turn of the century when the road level was lowered. This was the gathering place for the travelling shows that came to town. The twin-gabled building on the right is The British School, erected in 1852 by the Nonconformists to provide elementary education using the so-called Lancastrian system.

'Standing at the west or upper end of the High Street, is the Cross Inn [sic], whose existence as an hostelry, and indeed some of its present walls, dates back for at least 4 or 5 centuries. Facing down the High Street and next the corner shop, are two cottages; these are supposed to have been the former chapel of the Holy Cross. The walls and moulded timber roof above the ceiling indicate such a building.' (Robert Phillips, 1885.)

The former school buildings now occupied by two restaurants were Lilley & Skinner's shoe shop for many years; most people will remember the building nearby as The Pantry tearooms.

High Street, *c.* 1890. On the corner of Park Lane stood the shop belonging to Frank Russell & Co., wardrobe dealers.

Almost completely rebuilt in the 1900s, this scene is now overshadowed by the mass of 'street furniture' made necessary by the volume of traffic.

High Street, *c.* 1905. In the middle distance is the Congregational Church, erected in 1831, enlarged and re-fronted in stone in 1869 and accommodating 550 people. The porticoed entrance in the foreground leads to Joseph Freeman, physician & surgeon. In 1892 the *Illustrated Business Guide to Reigate, Redhill & Horley* stated: 'The town itself has a quiet well-to-do appearance. There are a number of handsome shops, and it is evident from the quality of the goods shewn, as well as from the number of gentlemen's residencies in the neighbourhood, that Reigate is a centre of considerable commercial activity, and happily combines rural charms with the practical advantages and conveniences of 19th. century town-life.'

Another ugly building has appeared, on the left, and the church has been replaced with a similarly unsympathetic block of shops/offices. Fortunately, the current boom in dining out has led to some very agreeable conversions, Caffé Uno and Tortellini/The Dining Room being two examples that are visible in this scene.

High Street, *c.* 1912. The fair is in town and has set up in its customary position at the western end, close to the Red Cross Inn. The stall in the foreground asks the intriguing question 'Have you seen Flossy?' Closer investigation reveals that Flossy has five legs and two tails and that he, she or it can be viewed for just tuppence.

Parked cars take the place of the fairground stalls; other than that, the buildings are much the same.

High Street, *c.* 1958. Two-way traffic and plenty of cars that we remember owning: Minis, Triumph Heralds, Austin A30s; and familiar shop names such as Appleby's, Dalton's, The Pantry, Bibby's and Rosa Hyett.

After a bleak period when many shops at the western end of the town closed, there seems to be something of a revival going on and many of the properties are looking smarter than they ever have been. The Nutley Gallery, Caffé Uno and Oddbins have all helped revive the fortunes of this part of the town, while on the other side of the street Brents Priory have taken on the business of The Pantry, and Marcus carries on the trade of tailor, something rare in today's high streets.

High Street, *c.* 1905. According to the *Reigate Directory* of 1891: 'The Town Hall, erected in 1708 and situated in the Market Place, on the site of an ancient chapel of St Thomas a Becket, is a plain edifice of red brick, surmounted by a turret containing a clock with four illuminated dials; it is now used for petty sessions and as a market room and also for meetings of the Town Council.' It is now widely accepted that the Town Hall was erected in 1728, the same year that the old Market Place at the western end of town was demolished. The corner chimneys were added in 1853 as part of extensive alterations carried out by Lord Somers, but they have since been removed.

On the left, Boots the chemist has replaced the shops formerly occupied by F. Holden, photographer, and Jas. Deane, stationer; on the right, a new block of shops was constructed at the time of the Safeway development, replacing those of John Lilley, butcher, Burgess & Inman, corn merchants and W. Llewellyn, ladies' tailor.

High Street, *c.* 1925. The group of people on the right are standing outside the Public Hall, 'the seat of an old established and flourishing Mechanics' (lately re-named Literary) Institute, of the Holmesdale Natural History and Fine Arts Club and its Museum. Lectures and meetings of various kinds are held here.' (Robert Phillips, 1885.)

High Street, *c.* 1907. The street is a picture of tranquillity compared with that of today. Most of the shop names are long-gone: Bishop's stationer & printer, Mark Dean's refreshment rooms; and the delivery cart is from Lucas & Son. Beyond the Town Hall can be seen the frontage of the White Hart Hotel.

High Street, *c.* 1950. The familiar names of Meyers greengrocers, MacFisheries, Inman's corn and seed merchants and James Walker the jewellers. A little further along were Betty Kirby's wool shop, Mason's dress shop and Wragg's cycle shop.

New shops were built as part of the Safeway development, yet they retained the carcass of the original buildings, possibly improving the overall look of the block. Alexanders have taken over the jewellers and have had a new clock hung in its old position. Good for them!

High Street, *c.* 1950. On the left of the picture Barratt's shoe shop is just being created from the remains of the Mellersh & Neale office. The bank has become Westminster Bank Ltd and Timothy Whites & Taylors was a landmark for many years.

In the early 1950s a branch of F. W. Woolworth was built and this traded until the 1980s; the building then remained empty for some time until the present occupants took up residence in the 1990s.

High Street *c.* 1895. Nickalls & Knight, watchmakers and jewellers, are listed in the *Kelly's Directory* of 1891 but the shop appears to be empty, Thomas Nickalls was also the postmaster so perhaps he moved when the 'new' post office was opened in Bell Street in 1895. A notice on the post office of 1891 proclaimed that 'Letters arriving from London and all parts are delivered at 7.15, 10.15, 2.45 and 6 p.m. on all weekdays, Sundays at 7.15 a.m. only.' Next door is the tailor's shop belonging to Alfred Knight, one of four traders of that surname in the town.

Alfred Knight's shop has remained intact, becoming a branch of the Home & Colonial Stores in the 1930s and now, after major rebuilding works to incorporate the neighbouring shop, it is a branch of the Blockbuster Video stores. White & Sons was formerly a tobacconist and tea merchant, while the recently created Abbey National branch was a baker and confectioners for many years.

The Swan, High Street, c. 1905. In the seventeenth century the town's principal hostelries were The Swan and The White Hart. By the middle of the nineteenth century The Swan was being labelled a 'commercial inn', while The White Hart was 'thoroughly well managed, and possesses accommodation of a superior order' (R.F.D. Palgrave, 1860). It was demolished in about 1938 along with the block of buildings surrounding it, including the shop to the right of The Swan which for many years was the premises of William Allingham, bookseller, referred to as The Library.

For most people of a certain age this building meant only one thing . . . the Court School of Dancing, which ran dance classes on the first floor. Others will remember the shops of Montague Burton, Walton's fruiterers and The International Tea Co.

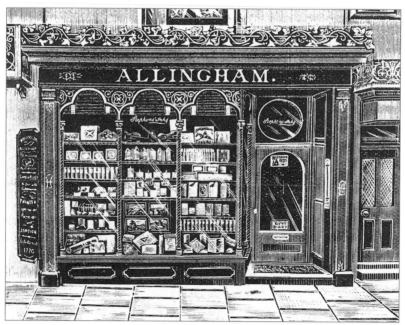

Allingham, bookseller. Market Place, 1897. 'The business was established in 1776 and has remained in the family ever since. Mr Allingham's stock is the largest and most exhaustive in the district, and he is fittingly recognised as the leading bookseller and stationer by the most aristocratic among the resident and visiting population of the town. Another important feature of the business is the printing branch which is well appointed and replete with every appliance. The proprietor has availed himself of every modern resource of the lithographic, steel and copperplate engraving, die-sinking and letterpress printing industry. His establishment is also a booking office for entertainments and the proprietor arranges seating and attendants for same if required.'

The Market Place was rebuilt in 1939, the left-hand portion being a branch of Montague Burton with Stanley Burton's foundation stone still visible by the doorway. Walton's fruiterers occupied this shop for some years, and after having lain empty for months it has recently become a branch of Toni & Guy, hairdressers.

Pither, brush manufacturer, Market Square, 1892. 'Mr Pither holds a very large and comprehensive stock of goods; which is replete with all the best features of various lines in this class of trade, embracing a most extensive assortment of brushes for general house use, butler's pantry, laundry, dairy, stable and toilet use, and a large and varied selection of mats and matting, baskets in great variety, suitable for domestic and tradesmen's use, and an immense assortment of miscellaneous articles.'

For many years this shop was Martin Dunsford, outfitters, and is now Gerrards.

High Street, *c.* 1905. Mellersh & Neale were established as brewers in Reigate by Thomas Neale in 1801, with an office at 19 High Street alongside the imposing London, County and Westminster Bank. Neale also started the first private bank in the town in Old Bank Buildings at the top of Bell Street; this venture failed in 1850. Opposite the brewery office was Mark Dean's Refreshment Rooms: 'large and small parties catered for, cyclists' rest.'

Only the bank building remains, adding a small sense of permanence to the scene. For many years the shop to the right of the bank was occupied by Timothy Whites and a Woolworths store. It now accommodates the ubiquitous high street stores Clinton's and Martin's.

CHAPTER THREE

REIGATE: CHURCH STREET

*Church Street, c. 1909. At this time there were only a small number of shops in the street, and behind the
wall on the left stood the large grounds of The White Hart Hotel, extending to three acres.*

F. W. Budgen, Market Place. 'Started by Alderman Budgen, father of F. W. Budgen, their price list and catalogue occupied 70 pages of printed matter, making it the largest and best of its kind in Reigate. When the public are having every species of dodgery practised upon them by vendors of cheap but unwholesome teas, Mr Budgen, like many another tradesman, purchases growths of the very best kinds, and by carefully blending the young leaves, is enabled to offer really good tea of excellent flavour and free from adulteration.'

The shop has had many occupants since 1897, including Adam's store, Tesco and several restaurants. Currently it is a branch of Café Rouge. On the first floor is the hairdressing salon of Paul Kelmsley which had previously been Barry Woolf's.

Town centre, *c.* 1940. This shows the town after its first major facelift; Wilfrid Hooper describes events and opinions in his 1945 *Reigate. Its Story through the Ages*: 'The most important event in the life of Reigate town since the war of 1914–1918 was the sale of the greater portion of it in 1921 by Mr Somers Somerset. This ended the long regime of single ownership and opened the way to sweeping alterations which have done much to change the face of the town. Chain shops built to stereotyped plans which pay no regard to the prevailing styles have invaded the street and its unity has been further marred by the introduction into old façades of incongruous features such as timber work with the false idea of giving them an enhanced air of antiquity.'

Hardly any change to the appearance of the buildings is obvious, nearly sixty years on. Unfortunately the ancient buildings that were swept away in the 1930s were replaced by fairly undistinguished 'corporation'-style architecture.

Church Street, *c.* 1904. The collection of buildings on the right had, for a long time since, been used as a maltings and as a brewery, but from the early 1800s it had been used as a flour and corn store. In the 1920s it was to become The Old Wheel Restaurant, much loved among local diners, and its demolition is a topic which still irks many.

The unprepossessing block of shops and offices on the south side of the street were built on the site of the grounds of The White Hart Hotel, on the opposite side The Old Wheel Restaurant was knocked down, to be replaced by a modern facsimile that neither pleases nor displeases. Rather, it just seems pointless when judged against what it replaced.

Church Street, 1950. The White Hart name has been used again, for a new hotel built just around the corner from its illustrious predecessor in Bell Street. The row of shops leading up to Bancroft Road have yet to be built.

Redland plc expanded their headquarters building in Castlefield Road to take in several properties in Church Street, and the replica of The Old Wheel has been completed. The shops on the left have been built on some of the land formerly belonging to The White Hart Hotel. All of these Redland properties are currently unoccupied owing to the firm's relocation.

Church Street, *c.* 1908. This row of old cottages stood at the northern end of the street just beyond the corn and flour store that by then was Larmer's. Just beyond the cottages and hidden from view was a house called The Hermitage, lived in by Col. Thornton; this altered and extended property is now John Powell's gun shop.

The houses in the centre of the earlier photograph have gone but the one on the left is recognisable as the Holmesdale Benefit Building Society's premises although it has been altered and extended; the attractive little house with shuttered windows, visible over the shoulder of the cyclist, is The Cottage. The offices in the distance replaced Church Street Garage which itself replaced some old houses.

Church Street, *c.* 1940. The Old Wheel Luncheon & Tea House seen as most people remember it; the property was formerly a corn and flour store, which in 1850 belonged to Edward Larmer, the miller at Wray Common windmill who also had a corn business in the Market Square. His son Arthur succeeded to the shop and store, later selling it to Farrington's. A wheel formerly projected over the footpath for the purpose of raising and lowering sacks of corn and it was this device that gave the building its name when it became a teahouse in 1926. The wheel used to hang on the wall inside the dining room of the teahouse.

The building that replaced The Old Wheel was supposed to replicate the original, externally at least.

Church Street, *c.* 1900. At this eastern end of the town there were only large houses; it wasn't until the 1930s that the row of shops on the southern side was constructed. The row of pollarded trees are outside The Baron's, built in 1710.

Bancroft and Castlefield Roads have been constructed, the shops on the south side of the street have been built, and the grand house on the right has been adapted by the former owners, Redland plc, for use as offices.

The Baron's, Church Street, *c.* 1910. Built in 1690 by London merchant Richard Devon, this fine Queen Anne-style mansion was subsequently purchased by the Somerset family and used as a dower house for the Priory. In around 1775 the house was purchased by Francis Maseres FRS, FSA, a former Attorney-General at Quebec who was made a Cursitor Baron of the Court of Exchequer, and thereafter the house became known as The Baron's. Maseres remained at the house for fifty years. During the course of the First World War Baron's was used as a GHQ and latterly split into apartments. In the 1920s Mr Alan Ely restored it to most of its former splendour, but much of that work was undone when the house became the base for a funeral director.

In the 1980s the building products company Redland plc, whose headquarters building faced The Baron's, purchased the house, demolished all of the nineteenth-century additions and lavished a great deal of effort and expense on recreating the house as it may have looked when it was built. In order to make greatest use of the property, they had much of the garden area asphalted for car parking. The house is, alas, empty at the time of publication, since the company has moved to the Midlands, and the former gardens/car park are being developed for housing.

Church Street, *c*. 1910. Elmshade was a grand mansion that occupied a large tract of land between Church Street and what is now Castlefield Road. Redland purchased the site for their new headquarters building.

The extension to the Redland offices in the 1980s makes a comparative photograph difficult as most of the site is now covered by the buildings.

Church Street. *c.* 1900. E.M. Ninnes, ironmonger, occupied these premises until they were demolished in 1901 to make way for Castlefield Road and the subsequent construction of the Municipal Buildings. The gateway on the right led to Reigate Lodge, a substantial building with 28 acres encompassing most of the land between Croydon Road to the east and Tunnel Road to the west. The Corporation purchased the site in 1911 with a view to developing it for housing and a new school, but work did not commence until after the First World War and the Lodge was demolished in 1922, making way for the County School for Girls and the housing in East Walk, South Walk, Rushworth Road, Orchard Road and Chart Way.

The site that was once occupied by a grand Victorian house called Elmshade became the headquarters for building supplies group Redland plc, which started trading as a producer of concrete tiles in Doods Road in 1919. As the company expanded, so too did Redland House, taking in properties along Church Street, and in the 1980s the large extension (seen left of centre) heralded the company's importance as a supplier to international markets with interests worldwide. In 1997 Redland was acquired by a French company, Lafarge, and the offices have been vacated leaving a new chapter to be written.

CHAPTER FOUR

REIGATE: BELL STREET

Bell Street, c. 1920. A horse waits outside Edwards's smithy and a little further on the newly established premises of The Reigate Garage Ltd provides tangible evidence of the threat that the motor vehicle was to prove to horse-power.

The White Hart Hotel, *c*. 1909. 'Round the Market Place are, as is usual, several old inns. The Swan has a last century market town appearance and was of yore the inevitable headquarters of the Parliamentary candidate who failed to obtain The White Hart, which, with its modern appointments, has very long held the rank of principal hotel. Here the lumbering stage changed horses, and its passengers got down, to the daily delectation of the waiters outside and dined to the gratification of the waiters inside.' (Robert Phillips, 1885.) This shows the stage coach 'The Venture', operated by millionaire Alfred Vanderbilt as a nostalgic enterprise, for the day of this form of transport had long since passed as a commercial exercise. Mr Vanderbilt's memory is honoured by a granite memorial which stands virtually unseen by the side of the A24 at Holmwood. The inscription reads: 'Alfred Gwynne Vanderbilt, a gallant gentleman and a fine sportsman who perished in the *Lusitania*, May 7th 1915. This stone is erected on his favourite road by a few of his British coaching friends and admirers.'

The hotel that had for so long been a symbol of the town's genteel prosperity was demolished in 1935 to be replaced by the block of shops/offices that we know today. The low-roofed building just beyond the 1930s block stands on the site of the ancient chapel of St Lawrence, one of three chapels which the town could boast in medieval times.

Bell Street, *c.* 1940. The White Hart has been replaced by a row of shops and flats and the street has already started to fill with motor cars. A traffic light stands outside the National Provincial Bank, opposite which are Lewis's (tobacconists) and Dorothy Perkins (ladies' clothes).

The shops on the left have all changed owners, with three currently unoccupied. The former bank building has lost its top storey and is now a branch of the Alliance & Leicester. There is a great deal more 'street furniture' cluttering up the scene, all of it a result of our car culture.

T.S. Marriage, ironmonger, 27 Bell Street, 1897. 'The principal display of goods is admirably and effectively arranged to catch the eye of the visitors immediately on entering the front shop. Here may be noticed many beautiful specimens of ornamental brass and copper goods, a large case containing electro-plated goods, sufficient in both quality and variety to satisfy the most fastidious taste. The workshops of the firm are situated to the rear of the premises, and give employment to a large number of hands. The work carried on is of a varied character to meet the requirements of a large and wide connection, and comprises range and hot water work of every description, wrought iron fencing of all kinds, installation and repair of electric bells and telephones, plumbing, gas-fitting and bell-hanging in all their various branches.'

Marriage's were at this site until the early 1960s; now it is a Chinese restaurant with a small barber's shop next door.

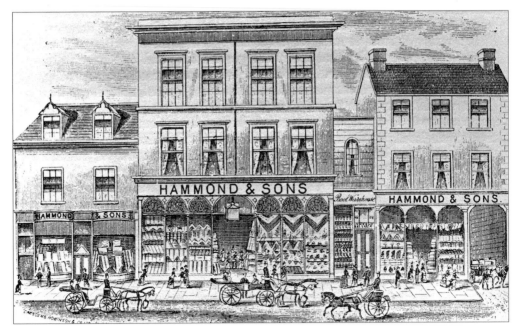

Hammond & Sons, draper, Bell Street, 1897. 'Turning to the dressmaking department, we may say at once that this important branch is under the direction of an experienced and clever first hand. The utmost care is taken in falling in with the wishes of customers, and all things considered, it is not matter of much wonder that Messrs. Hammond & Sons enjoy the patronage of so many of the ladies resident in the town, who, from experience, know it to be unnecessary to travel to London for costumes, which, as regards fit, style and excellence of make, can be obtained at home and which would be difficult to obtain elsewhere.'

The building on the right became the Palace Picturedrome in 1912, later the Hippodrome, and was demolished in the 1960s to be replaced by a car showroom and offices. The shop on the left was formerly Sydney Bailey, outfitter.

Mellersh & Neale, 1897: 'This brewery has been established for nearly a century and although it does not possess any architectural beauty, it is commodious, and of late years, in order to meet the requirements of the times and increasing trade, large sums of money have been laid out in the procuring of the latest modern appliances, with which it is well equipped. It also has the great advantage of possessing a supply of pure chalk water, running from springs at the base of Reigate Hill to the brewery.'

Perhaps the greatest upheaval to the town in recent years was the Safeway development, constructed on the former brewery yard and other areas of public car park. Open seven days a week, the store has proved to be highly successful, but whether the town as a whole has benefited remains a moot point.

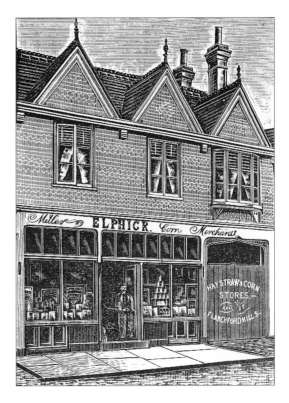

Edward Elphick, miller, hay, straw and corn merchant, Bell Street, 1897. 'The old established and important business of Mr Elphick, carried on at Bell Street and at Flanchford mills, is one of the most extensive in the borough. The premises occupied are favourably situated, regarded from every point of view. They are sufficiently extensive to meet the demands of so large a connection as the proprietor enjoys, and comprise large and commodious stores where extensive stocks are kept and as Mr. Elphick buys in the best markets for cash, he is in a position to offer special advantages to his customers, especially so in regard to English oats.'

This shop fell victim to the building of Bancroft Road.

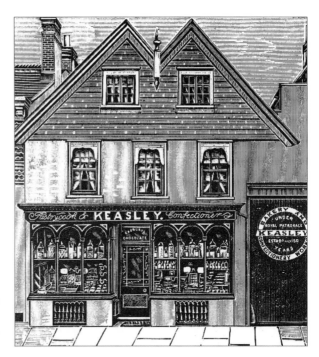

Keasley & Sons, confectioners, Bell Street, 1897. 'Reigate can boast of having, amongst other remarkable things, one of the oldest established confectionery businesses in the British Isles. Confectionery is said to be the poetry of eating, and for 150 years the wants of the inhabitants of the town and district in this respect have been supplied by the family so worthily represented today by Messrs. Keasley & Sons of Bell Street. It is their privilege to be under the patronage of their Royal Highnesses the Prince & Princess of Wales, as well as that of the nobility and gentry of the surrounding district.'

The construction of Bancroft Road in 1936 meant the demolition of the old-established bakery.

Bell Street, *c.* 1890. At the far end of the street is the Forge House and Edwards's smithy, and the row of trees marks the site where the 'new' post office will shortly be. Between the two sites, T. Marriage had his hardware shop which later became Reigate Garage Ltd.

The finishing touches are just being added to the new set of office buildings on the triangular plot left vacant after the Safeway development was completed.

Bell Street, *c.* 1905. Wilfrid Hooper writes: 'In 1895, through the efforts of some of the local tradesmen, the present [post office] building in Bell Street was erected on ground leased by Lady Henry Somerset, the free-hold of which has since been acquired by the Crown.' Next door is Northover's, cabinet makers and house furnishers; next to them is the saddlery shop of William Lanaway.

The Safeway development caused the most change to the town since the 1930s. The block of buildings which included the 'new' post office were knocked down to allow for the entrance road to the superstore. Part of the changes in the 1930s included the construction of Bancroft Road upon which stood the Majestic cinema, owned by S. King and H. Bancroft, the latter of whom also owned the Hippodrome on Bell Street which started life in 1912 as the Palace Picturedrome. There was also a Majestic swimming pool opposite the cinema, an open-air lido-style affair, which closed in the 1960s to be replaced by Pool House.

Bell Street, *c*. 1900. The Forge House and smithy of Edwards, farriers and shoeing smiths since 1795.

The Forge House remains intact and is now offices, but the smithy has gone and has been replaced by a building with the appearance of having been there longer than its years.

Bell Street, *c.* 1910. Behind the tree on the left is the stables entrance to The Priory and just beyond that is the forge, which is presumably where the boy has just taken his horse. A little further down the street, by the small tree, is the row of shops containing the post office.

The public car park entrance is the former Priory stable access, and Finch & Son's cycle shop, which opened in 1926 at this site, operates from no. 43 with a new façade spanning across to no. 41, Surf & Ski sports equipment shop.

Bell Street, *c*. 1905. The horse with a nose-bag is standing outside the premises of James Keasley & Sons, old-established baker & confectioner.

In 1935 Bancroft Road was built, relieving some of the congestion at the Old Town Hall traffic lights; and so, after more than 150 years, Keasley's ceased trading.

Bell Street, *c.* 1960. The road is busy with what are now 'period' cars. The showroom for Reigate Garage is on the left, founded in 1908, and opposite is the old established cycle shop B. Finch & Son. Reigate Galleries have established their business next door to Martin Graham's jeweller's shop.

The Reigate Garage building went to make way for the entrance to Safeway along with the block of shops containing the old post office. On the other side of the road, however, there is some sense of permanence with Reigate Galleries, Finch's and Martin Graham's all still trading in the same premises.

Priory gates, *c.* 1878. The splendid main entrance to Reigate's largest house featured stone eagles atop majestic columns supporting wrought-iron gates. The small brick archway, extreme right in the picture, is reputedly Tudor, constructed when the Priory was held by Lord William Howard after the Dissolution of the monasteries. The gates, with their eagles, were ordered to be removed to the rear of the building by Lady Henry Somerset, who took exception to a public house (The Castle) being built opposite. Few plots of land in the town did not belong to the Somersets but this was one of them; thus she had no direct control over the proposed building.

Where the gates once stood, buses now stand. Behind the wall is a very popular children's playground and near the public car-park entrance is a row of small headstones erected to the memory of beloved pets that roamed freely in the grounds when they were in private ownership.

Reigate Priory, *c*. 1920. Lord Somers purchased the estate in 1808; it remained with the family until 1921 when Mr Somers Somerset sold it to Countess Beatty, wife of Admiral of the Fleet, Earl Beatty. Upon her death it passed to her younger son Mr Peter Beatty, who was to become the last private owner of the Priory.

Sold in 1942 to the Mutual Property Life and General Insurance Co. Ltd, in 1945 the Priory was acquired by the Reigate Borough Council for use as a community centre and playing fields. In the 1960s and early 1970s the house was Reigate Priory Secondary School; it later became Priory Middle School, one of the largest in the county.

Reigate Priory from the Park *c.* 1910. Founded in the early half of the thirteenth century by William de Warrenne, fifth Earl of Surrey, as a small house of Augustinian monks, it was initially a hospital. By the end of the century it was purely a religious institution deemed to be the least wealthy of any in Surrey; after the Dissolution the last Prior, John Lymden, was granted a pension of £10 per annum. Henry VIII granted the Priory to William Howard, 1st Lord Effingham. It is thought that in converting the building into a private residence he swept away most of the original monastery.

The façade of the Priory is much the same, but the formal gardens have gone save for a small sunken garden in front of what is now the school hall. Local sports enthusiasts enjoy the facilities provided for playing tennis, football and cricket.

Park Gate, *c*. 1907. In his *Illustrated Handbook to Reigate*, R.F.D. Palgrave recounts the words of the Village Chronicler: 'On Reigate Heath, about eighty-six years ago (circa 1729), a man known by the nickname of Roley-Poley, was hanged in chains for the murder of Mr Coecock (a farmer at Ifield), about seven o'clock in the evening, near the Park Gate. He laid in waiting for a Mr Charington, who was a very sober, steady man, and always rode very slow, but having that evening drunk more than common, he rode very fast, which saved his life. Mr Coecock coming by soon after, very slow, Roley-Poley shot him, and rifled his pockets. The murderer was taken a day or two afterwards at Epsom; and he was tried and found guilty, upon the evidence of a servant girl, who was in bed with his wife when he returned home, and saw the watch, and money, which he had brought with him.'

The Priory Gate still stands but is used little, for it offers access onto the constantly busy Cockshott Hill, whereas a small diversion along a footpath to the left leads to a stretch of road where a traffic island enables safer crossing for those many people who use the Park for exercising themselves and their dogs.

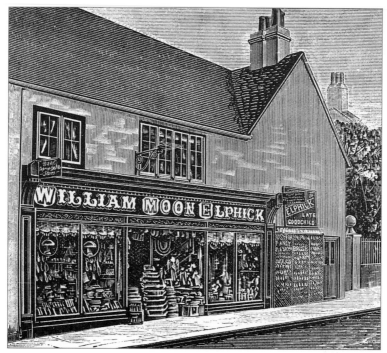

Broom Hall, Bell Street, 1897. 'Next to the castle itself, there is no other building in Reigate can compete with Broom Hall in antiquity. This old building has stood for 400 years, and is a notable object in Bell Street, being situated exactly opposite the residence of Lady Somerset. For some 60 years past, the business of brush and basket maker and cooper has been and is still carried on here, where goods of the best manufacture may be had, but the proprietor has recently added a fancy bazaar. Mr Elphick, builder & contractor, has acquired Broom Hall and converted his property into a grand bazaar, where, besides a multitude of minor articles, household requisites of every description can be purchased at very moderate charges.'

Well-known local businesses Knight's and Northover's have both used this building until in 1931 Arthur Cole started the Ancient House Library and Café, which is now a bookshop. The southern gable was knocked down to create access to the rear for a car repair shop. The block of shops and offices on the right are built on the site of the house called Holmfels.

Bell Street, *c.* 1932. Arthur Cole acquired the property from Northovers and started the Ancient House Library and Café, the latter enterprise being on the first floor.

The Ancient House Bookshop is still trading under the same name after sixty-seven years in the same premises, and for half that period Sean Hawkins has been working at the shop, which he now owns.

Bell Street, *c.* 1905. J. Northover has premises on both sides of the street. On the right is his furniture showroom and undertaker's office; on the other side of the road next to the post office he has his cabinet-making workshop. Just beyond the row of trees, T. Marriage, who has an established ironmongery at 21 Bell Street, has moved with the times and established Reigate Garages Ltd at no. 20.

The Ancient House Bookshop has replaced Northover's, with part of the fine old building having been demolished to create an access to the car repair workshops at the rear. The bookshop first appears in *Kelly's Directory* in 1931 listed as the Ancient House Library and Café, managing director Mr Arthur Cole.

Bell Street, *c.* 1910. Henry Guy's tobacconist's shop is at the centre of the picture and the vehicle is parked outside Tamplin & Makovski's premises.

There is very little similarity here, with most of the buildings having undergone some degree of change. In the foreground are two of Reigate's popular restaurants, La Barbe and La Lanterna.

Bell Street, *c.* 1925. Outside The Castle Inn stand two solid-tyred lorries carrying sand or aggregate, and outside Tamplin & Makovski's is a milk cart belonging to S. Hawkins of Meadvale. On the far left of the picture is Dean's tearooms, also situated by the Town Hall.

Road haulage is still evident but of a vastly different shape and size. The tearooms might be remembered by some as the Tudor Bell Restaurant or La Ronde café, in the 1960s, where one could buy a wonderful invention called espresso coffee which was always served in clear glass cups and saucers. Today it is a popular Italian restaurant, La Lanterna.

Bell Street, *c*. 1920. The sign declaring 'Motor Garage' is the premises of Tamplin & Makovski who were electrical engineers, but for a period they also described themselves as automobile engineers. Beyond that is The Reigate Press works (out of sight) and Henry Guy's house, from which he ran a tobacconist's and a building and decorating business.

The bracket for Tamplin & Makovski's hanging sign remains, but the building is now offices and most of the shops beyond have been built since 1930.

CHAPTER FIVE

REIGATE: THE SURROUNDING DISTRICTS

South Park, c. 1908. The name South Park is thought to have been adopted in the 1870s, by which time the National Freehold Land Society had begun to build houses on land owned by the Gander family since about 1580. Crescent Road leads off to the left and the track on the right was supposedly used by carters because it had a lesser gradient.

Park Lane East, *c.* 1908. Known at this period as Light Hill, possibly because it was gas-lit, the lodge house to Park House is on the left. On the right, at the junction with Priory Road, stands The Holmesdale public house.

The name Light Hill has fallen into disuse, with the road now called Park Lane East. On the left, new bungalows have been built on the former field; opposite, new blocks of flats have risen. The Holmesdale was demolished in the late 1980s and several houses have been shoe-horned into the site.

Allingham Road, South Park, *c.* 1912. The foundation stones for the Congregational Church were laid by Lady Henry Somerset (of the Priory) and Mr W. Tyndall in 1889 and the church opened in September of that year. A classroom and schoolroom were added in 1893 with provision for 150 children. Next door, the post office is accommodated in Hood's draper's shop.

The church is now widely used by the Christadelphians and local groups; the post office is run by Mrs Janet Wool and her son David, who also sell stationery and greetings cards. Before the Wools arrived in 1988 the shop had been run for thirty years by Mr and Mrs Runacres and their daughter Eileen.

Cockshott Hill, *c.* 1910. This area had long been associated with the manufacturing of pottery, and a site described as Potteriches on the west side of Cockshott Hill was mentioned in a survey of 1623. There was a small brickyard and pottery in this area until the early 1900s.

Some houses have now been built in the lane named Old Pottery Close and the A217 takes an increasingly heavy load of traffic, with the continuing growth of Gatwick Airport being a contributory factor.

Cronks Hill, Meadvale, *c.* 1912. The name supposedly derives from a meadow associated with Henry Cranke in the fifteenth century. Most of the houses seen here are Victorian or Edwardian, having been built by the National Freehold Land Society or its auxiliary, The British Land Company, which were formed in 1849.

On 21 September 1940: 'Soon after 8 p.m. a single aeroplane was heard passing northwards and a minute or two before 9, two bombs came shrieking down in the Meadvale district. One exploded on a roadside bank, causing trees and earth to block the Cronks Hill Road. A passing 447 bus came in for some rough mauling. The blast damaged at least 13 houses in the road.' (Charles Preston, *The Borough of Reigate in Wartime 1939–1945.*)

An abundance of conifers masks some of the original houses.

Meadvale, Lower Road, *c.* 1910. Until early in the nineteenth century this area was referred to as Mead Hole; until relatively recently bricks and earthenware were made here by Messrs W. Brown & Sons, at whose works a pit of Atherfield clay was dug for over 100 years. 'The Atherfield Clay shrinks less on drying, but is not so strong as the Weald Clay, which has a large shrinkage. Atherfield Clay with an admixture of Wealden Clay is used here for making the tiles and pots, while the Wealden Clay mixed with sand is used for brickmaking. One million bricks per year is considered a good output from these works.' (*The Geology of the County around Reigate & Dorking*, Dines & Edmundson, 1933.) The Primitive Methodist Church, on the left, was built in 1855.

The church is still functioning and, despite the addition of some telegraph poles and a bit of modern in-filling, the scene is not vastly different from that of ninety years ago.

Croydon Road, *c.* 1920. This road was created in 1808, 'thus affording a new and improved route to the metropolis, and diverting the traffic from the former turnpike over Banstead Downs and Reigate Hill'. (Robert Phillips, *A Geographical, Historical and Topographical Description of the Borough of Reigate & Surrounding District*, 1885.) The substantial Victorian houses were built following the success of the railway and the link that it provided with business in London. At the southern end of the road are the premises occupied by Holmesdale Natural History Club, founded in 1857 and still going strong. R.F.D. Palgrave described the club in 1860 thus: 'The study of Natural History is ably forwarded by the "Holmesdale Club"; an association of about seventy members, mostly residents here, under the presidency of Mr Wilson Saunders. The object of the Club, the investigation of the Natural History of the surrounding Country, is pleasantly fulfilled by many summer excursions. Mr Evelyn has shewn true liberality in entertaining the Club at Wotton, with a ready kindness that made his welcome a welcome indeed, and other gentlemen blessed with extensive grounds in that lovely region about Dorking, have done the like.'

Such capacious houses remain popular but the growth in ownership of cars has meant that some road-width has had to been given over for parking.

Glovers Road, *c.* 1909. The roads in this part of town were developed on a parcel of land named Glovers Field after the owner, Ambrose Glover FSA, a local solicitor and historian of high repute who had contributed the larger part of the matter relating to the Reigate Hundred in Manning and Bray's *County History*.

Very little has changed in this street and the well-proportioned Victorian houses remain popular family homes.

Smoke Lane, *c*. 1910. This little lane, off Cockshott Hill, is possibly named after the charcoal burning industry that was associated with this area in earlier times. Earlswood, Wray Common and Woodhatch were heavily wooded until the seventeenth century. The house, called Rosebank, was occupied by the Revd Calvin Martin in 1891.

Rosebank is now divided into two residences and the lane itself is a footpath.

The Angel Inn, Woodhatch, *c*. 1935. This photograph was taken at a time when there was insufficient traffic on the A217 to warrant traffic lights at the Prices Lane junction.

The view is partially obscured now by the enormous road-sign, many of which have been erected recently throughout the country with little regard for their ugly intrusion upon rural landscapes.

The Angel Inn, Woodhatch, *c.* 1904. Pevsner said of this building in 1962: 'On the main road south of the town is The Angel, Woodhatch, a very queer half-timbered building and almost like a folly. Very tall and thin three deep storeys and a gable with two lean-tos giving the effect of a clerestory. Regular timbering, possibly of *c.* 1650. Oddly deliberate and formal especially for south-east England.' In the eighteenth century the building became an inn called The White Horse, changing to its present name in 1814.

The old inn stands at this busy crossroads, seemingly marooned in an endless flow of traffic. A tower crane can be seen to the left, working on the reconstruction of the former Crusader Insurance site (formerly Woodhatch Lodge).

Nutley Lane, *c.* 1905. According to the *Kelly's Directory* of 1891, 'The Mission Church in Nutley Lane, attached to the church of St Mark, was erected and endowed in 1864 at the sole expense of the late William Philipps Esq., and has sittings for about 300 persons, the curacy has an endowment of £120 yearly, with residence, and held since 1889 by Rev. David Marshal Lang M.A. of Corpus Christi College, Cambridge.'

In earlier times this lane was the main northern access to the town, particularly for the many pilgrims making their way to the shrine of Thomas à Becket at Canterbury Cathedral and who sought shelter and sustenance for their onward journey. R.F.D. Palgrave pictured the scene: 'What troops of wayfarers during each successive summer, crowded these quiet streets of Reigate, flocking down from the hills when the long shadows were glancing eastward up the Valley, all dusty and footsore into the Town; the Irish, Welsh, and Normans, perplexing the Innkeepers by their questions in French and Celtic. What a sight Nutley Lane must then have presented.'

In 1991 a resolution was passed separating St Philip's (the old Mission Church) from its sister church St Mark's in Alma Road, and it now serves its own parish.

E. Penfold, monumental mason, Lesbourne Road, 1897. 'Under the guidance and direction of Messrs. Penfold, the storied urn or animated bust is treated as it deserves to be. Carving in marble or stone has in this establishment achieved a distinct success; crosses, figures, tablets, tombs and monuments are constructed with care and precision, the chief aim being to produce works of art reliable, durable and of highly-furnished workmanship.'

In more recent times Northover & Sons used the premises for the monumental masonry aspect of their funerary business which was based at The Baron's, in Church Street, but for some time now the building, on its island site, has housed a ladies' clothes shop.

Lesbourne Road, *c.* 1910. One of Mellersh & Neale's public houses was Lesbourne Hall, the 'hall' portion of the name being a title that was given to establishments which could offer simple overnight accommodation for the working classes whose pockets could not stretch to the cost of a hotel. This title is also found locally in Nutley Hall, in Nutley Lane.

The exterior of the pub has had the mock-Tudor treatment but the new name is a little removed from that period: The Desert Rat.

St. Mark's Church, Alma Road, *c.* 1908. R.F.D. Palgrave mentions this proposed church in his 1860 *Handbook to Reigate*: 'The foundation of St Mark's Church, Wray Park, on a site about two hundred yards to the North of the railway station, is a step towards meeting the religious requirements of this increasing Parish. It is intended to afford 720 sittings, one third free, and to cost, with the parsonage house, £5, 600.' The church was erected in 1860 and enlarged four years later.

The spire, found to be unstable, was removed in 1918. The vicarage was demolished recently and replaced with one of a smaller, modern design in 1971. The road itself has recently been introduced to the benefits of 'traffic-calming' humps on its surface.

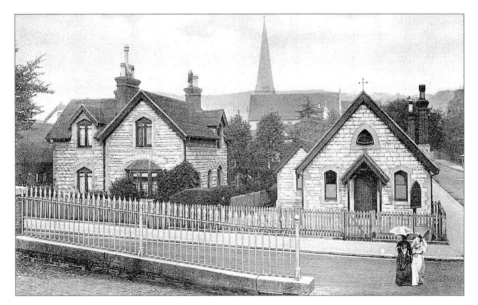

St Mark's School, *c.* 1912. Photographed from the forecourt of the railway station, this looks down Alma Road towards St Mark's Church. The school was built in 1869 to accommodate 300 children. The area was described in 1881 thus: 'Where once were fields and untrimmed hedgerows now are villas and shops, railroads and carriage-roads, and all the improvements which follow in the wake of civilization. The park [Wray Park] retains the name only of what it once was, as it is now dotted over with pretty detached residences. The model dairy-farm and breeding establishment for Jersey cattle, belonging to G. Simpson Esq., is situated in this part, also St Mark's Church & School etc.' (*Half-holiday Handbooks. Round Reigate.* Marshall, Japp & Co.)

After the demolition of the school buildings the site was developed for industrial use, and for a long period this was both workshop and training facilities for the Royal National Institute for the Blind, latterly becoming vehicle repair workshops for the Council. These apartments were constructed in the 1990s.

Castle Grounds, c. 1880. This splendid photograph was taken by noted Redhill photographer Edwin Dann and shows the Gardener's Lodge, which lies to the rear of the Municipal Buildings on a splendid site overlooking the roofs of the town. The whiskered gent is probably George Crutchfield.

The cottage still sits perched above the town but is in rather a poor state of repair. The upper windows have been replaced and the pretty diamond tiling has become plain tiles. The front garden is overgrown and this view is the best that could be achieved without the aid of an axe.

Holmesdale Road, *c.* 1914. The South Eastern Railway opened its Reading to Reigate line in 1849 and this road grew alongside the increasingly popular station. The whole area was then called Wray Park.

Very little has changed here; some housing has been built, but most of the buildings remain original. Of course, parked cars are a problem in such a narrow road – nothing unusual in 1998. In September 1940 'a bomb burst a few feet from the railway line, damaging a train standing in the station, and 64 houses and shops were damaged in various degrees'. (Charles Preston, *The Borough of Reigate in Wartime 1939–1945*.)

Park Lane, *c*. 1904. At the point where the photographer is standing there once was a workhouse, opened in 1730, and this stretch of the lane was thereafter referred to as Workhouse Lane, later being more attractively titled Park Pond Lane. The building at the top of the lane, facing the Red Cross Inn, is one of the sites of Frank Russell's wardrobe shop.

The butcher's shop at the top of the street is still trading. In 1891 it was William Watkins; in 1998 it is Markwick & Watson. The wardrobe dealer's shop is much enlarged and altered and now lies empty, since the Pierre Victoire restaurant group went into receivership.

Green Lane (Park Lane), 1920. 'Curious things to a minute philosopher are these same hollow lanes. They set him on archaeological questions, more than he can solve; and I meditate as I go, how many centuries it took to saw through the warm sandbanks of this dyke ten feet deep, up which he trots, with the oak boughs meeting over his head. Was it ever worth men's while to dig out the soil? Surely not. The old method must have been to remove the soft upper spit, till they got to tolerably hard ground; and then, Macadam's metal being as yet unknown, the rains and the wheels of generations sawed gradually deeper and deeper, till this road ditch was formed. But it must have taken centuries to do it.' (*Kingsley's Miscellanies*, vol. 1.)

The steps cut into the hillside are still popular with today's walkers; cars can be parked on the small lay-by opposite. Littleton Lane was the site of the eighteenth-century pest-house. On or near the same site, in 1859, the town's first public water supply was provided by the Reigate Water Works Company. Down the lane a short way is a pleasant footpath that leads to The Skimmington Castle on Reigate Heath.

Wray Common windmill, *c.* 1930. Built in 1824 on 'manorial waste', this 45 ft high tower mill was constructed of brick with walls 18 in thick; it operated four double-shuttered spring patent sails and a six-bladed fantail. It was depicted working in a magazine published in 1898, making it the last of the Reigate windmills to function; there are, however, reports of it having ceased operation in 1895. In about 1850 the miller was Edward Larmer, who also ran a corn business in the Market Square and had a corn and flour store in Church Street which was passed on to Mr Farrington and eventually became The Old Wheel Restaurant. By 1928 the windmill had been fitted with four shutterless dummy sails; by 1956 the tower had been given over to housing calves, fowls and hay on two of its five floors.

The sails have gone completely now, as has the fantail, but the main structure of the mill is sound and serving very well as a residence.

Wray Common, 1912. This impressive Edwardian mansion called Wray Mill House was constructed in 1911 for Robert Lemon, formerly of Wraylands, on the site of a house called Stoneyfield. Norman Walker, managing director of the British General Insurance Company, bought the house in 1924, remaining there until 1951. The house was then divided into four dwellings, all spacious, since the mansion originally comprised around twenty bedrooms, a smoking-room, billiard room, several reception rooms and, of course, servants' quarters.

Wray Mill House was demolished in 1988 and this development of thirty-eight luxury apartments in three blocks was built in its place.

Evesham Road, *c.* 1890. These old buildings were already derelict when this photograph was taken and were probably redundant agricultural structures. In the 1891 *Kelly's Directory* only three buildings are listed in this road: no. 1 belonged to William Egerton Hines, artist and art teacher at Harrow School; Kilmarnock to Eustace Fitzgerald; and Micklefield to William Read.

In September 1940, 'At 11 p.m. two bombs fell almost in the heart of Reigate at the junction of Evesham Road and West Street about 30 yards from a house where there were Soldiers of a Canadian Regiment. Two soldiers standing in the road were injured.' (Preston, *Reigate in Wartime. 1939–1945.*) It is extremely difficult to be accurate with this modern-day view as there is nothing left that gives a clue to the original location.

Reigate Heath, *c.* 1905. Children are able to play contentedly at the roadside, safe in the knowledge that the only disturbance they might suffer will come from an approaching horse and cart. In the middle distance is the Black Horse Inn, an eighteenth-century building that has been an inn since about 1785.

The road alignment was changed for traffic joining the busy A25 from Flanchford Road; this has significantly reduced the number of accidents at this junction. The opening of the final stretch of the M25 took a huge strain off this former main east–west route.

Reigate Heath, *c.* 1912. The heath was the venue for horse-racing between 1834 and 1838, and revived in 1863, but the meeting proved unpopular with the townspeople on account of the undesirable characters it attracted. In 1881 *Half-holiday Handbooks, Round Reigate* waxed lyrical about the area: 'The locality is often recommended to persons suffering from lung or chest complaints, its favourable situation in the Holmesdale valley rendering it suitable for those afflicted in this way. The Registrar's returns speak well for the sanitary condition of the borough, the death rate being only 13 per 1,000 in a combined population of nearly 20,000 not including outlying districts.'

The cottages on the Heath are still very popular, looking very much the way they did ninety years ago. Over the road, the open space is regularly used for cricket and football matches and a special track has been provided for horse-riding.

Heath Church, *c.* 1912. There is a degree of confusion over the precise details of the origins of this 'Iron Church'. Built on land donated by Mr E.G. Nash and erected through the generosity of local benefactors including Sir George Livesey and Mr F.N. Horne, the Heath Church was regarded as a daughter church to St Mary's and the first service was conducted by Vivian Banham on 28 July 1907.

There were several other examples locally of this style of church, which by the middle of the last century was being mass-produced and exported to America, South Africa and Australia. They were early examples of flat-pack technique. Leigh, Beare Green, Forest Green, Pixham and Newdigate all had iron churches indeed the one at Newdigate still stands, and has been used as a scout hut for many years.

In the summer months it is very difficult to see the church from the Flanchford road as the willow trees have grown unchecked and are rather unsightly. The building remains in sound condition and still attracts a regular monthly congregation. This interesting example of an iron church is now on the List of Buildings of Local Architectural and Historic Interest.

Reigate Heath, *c.* 1908. The heath has been dominated by its windmill since around 1765; for the first half of the nineteenth century Michael Bowyer ran this and nearby Wonham watermill. The sails stopped turning in 1868, and by 1880 the roundhouse had been converted into a chapel of ease to St Mary's Parish Church and named St Cross chapel after the chantry chapel of that name that stood in the High Street, near the Red Cross Inn.

The view across to the windmill is now obscured by the growth of trees, and two car parks have been created to accommodate the many dog owners who favour the light, sandy soil for wet day perambulations.

Reigate Heath, *c*. 1905. This whole area was very much the domain of the Bonny family. Robert was running The Skimmington Castle while his brother Alfred was running the mineral water factory, situated behind the house on the left called, naturally, Bonny Cottage. This had been built in 1901, by James Bonny who later had the bungalow and the row of ten cottages built, behind the factory, to house the employees. The factory made principally ginger beer and lemonade and delivered as far as Westerham, Capel and Burgh Heath in their wagons emblazoned with the motto 'Whilst I live I crow' above the emblem of a cockerel.

The mineral water business closed in the 1950s and the house and factory were sold. New homes have been built on the site of the factory; many of the cottages, all of which were originally owned by members of the Bonny family, have been sold. Trees and scrub have invaded the scene now and a road leads straight up to The Skimmington Castle, which is now out of sight.

Reigate Heath, *c.* 1900. The Skimmington Castle on the Heath has long been associated with the name of Bonny. James Bonny was the landlord in the last part of the nineteenth century and he was succeeded by his son Robert. The cottage to the left of the inn was let to agricultural workers and at one time housed as many as seven children.

The little cottage has been demolished and the inn has been much altered and extended. The access road has recently had all its pot-holes filled in, and a new car park has been constructed at the rear of the inn, making the little tavern more popular than ever.

Reigate Heath, *c.* 1912. The freehold of the club house, the mill and the miller's cottage were purchased by the Reigate Heath Golf Club in 1900. In 1943 the sails were blown down and were not replaced until the council bought the mill in 1960 and set about renovating the structure. By 1964 the programme had been completed with the mill having been re-tarred and with new sails, tail-pole and steps fitted.

In 1926 a sail broke and £360 was raised toward the cost of repairs. In 1997 also a sail broke and is awaiting repair; it will be interesting to see how much the repair costs seventy-one years on. In its original form the mill was fitted with four shutterless sail frames with provision for double shutters, and had a large striking wheel at the rear.

CHAPTER SIX

REDHILL

High Street, c. 1912. The name of outfitters Gatland's was familiar at this time as was that of Lipton's, the grocers, opposite.

High Street, *c.* 1935. At the corner of Cromwell Road stands The Tower public house, beyond which is Jones & Son drapers and soft furnishers and S.C. Jennings & Sons stationers.

There have been several name changes at the pub; when this photograph was taken it was called The Office but has since changed to a very rural-sounding Dog & Duck.

High Street, *c.* 1940. Some of the shops in this scene will be readily remembered by many people today, names such as Grice's bakery, Walton's fruiterers and Foster Brothers' clothes. These are all on the right of the picture.

The pedestrians-only High Street of 1998 bears little resemblance to that of 1940 except for that cluster of shops leading to the junction with Station Road. The Belfry Centre now looms large over the scene.

The Market Hall, *c.* 1906. At a public meeting in 1857 it was resolved 'that the population of Redhill and its immediate neighbourhood and the facilities of railway transit there, require that accommodation for a market should be provided and that a market house and conveniences including public rooms, should be built'. And so it was that in 1860 the Redhill Market House Co. Ltd was formed and proceeded to erect a prominent building upon a boggy piece of land known as Rough Moors. The site lived up to its name and piles had to be driven into the ground to support the structure. The west and east wings were added in 1891 and 1903 respectively and these housed the post office, county court and various societies. At the rear of the Hall was the Market Field, with a house, exclusively for the purpose of a market.

Redhill's 'grand plan' was executed in 1982, and many of the Victorian and Edwardian buildings were demolished to make way for the Warwick Quadrant which houses shops, the Harlequin Theatre, the library, a Sainsbury store and a large office complex. Unfortunately it also houses hundreds of pigeons which, despite valiant attempts by the council to deter them, still manage to cover the building with evidence of their occupancy.

High Street, *c.* 1920. On the left is the corner of the Market Hall, built in 1860 and enlarged in 1891 and 1903 to accommodate the post office, county court and societies. At the junction with Station Road stands the ladies' outfitters Nicol & Sons and on the opposite side of the High Street is The Wheatsheaf, built in 1900 for the brewers Nalder & Collyer.

Warwick Quadrant now dominates the scene where once stood the Market Hall, and the whole area has been given over to pedestrians.

Feldwick Place, London Road, 1980. This little lane led through to Cecil Place and comprised a row of six houses on the south side and six in Cecil Terrace on the north side They had gone before this photograph was taken but St Anne's still stands proud on the skyline.

Because of the looming presence of the Warwick Quadrant it is very difficult to be precise about the exact viewpoint today, but this is approximately the same spot.

London Road, *c.* 1920. Clarendon Road joins just to the left and at the corner is the Victoria Wine Co. On the other side of the road is The Sultan public house and a little further on is the garage of G. Linter & Sons.

Nothing remains today of this part of London Road except for a small portion of the Memorial Sports Ground.

London Road, *c.* 1912. Sir Jeremiah Colman, of Gatton Park, had the Colman Institute erected in 1904 primarily to house the town's Literary Institution, founded in 1884.

Hardly anything remains of the Edwardian London Road; Warwick Quadrant has replaced the Colman Institute and also swallowed up part of the Memorial Sports Ground which was home to Redhill FC, founded in 1894 and now languishing on a scrappy site in Earlswood.

London Road, *c.* 1912. 'In June 1846 a large quantity of land was leased for 99 years by the trustees of Lord Monson. This land extended from Frenches Gate to the bridleway in the lane crossing the High Street and, in the other direction, from near Oxford Road almost to the railway, except a small portion adjoining the crossing of Station Road. This stimulated building and houses were erected in Warwick Road, Station Road, High Street and Grove Road. These were mostly small and the latter of that class that induces squalor and slum-life. A few larger houses were built in the London Road and Linkfield Lane.' (Phillips, *A Geographical, Historical and Topographical Description of Reigate and Surrounding Districts*, 1885.)

Very few of the Victorian houses remain along London Road today.

Station Road, *c.* 1950. Nicol's store suffered an horrific fire in 1901 and the building was destroyed, claiming two lives. The shop was rebuilt in typically lavish Edwardian style and later became a branch of Burton, the tailors. John Nicol continued trading in smaller premises in Station Road until the 1960s.

Many shops have come and gone in the old Nicol's store, but The Wheatsheaf and the bank remain substantially unaltered. The pub has just been renovated, falling foul of the theming epidemic that has swept through the large brewery chains, and they would now like it to be known as 'The Firlot & Firkin'. The whole area is now paved.

Station Road, *c.* 1910. 'The town owes its present importance to the fact of its being a junction for the South Eastern & London, Brighton and South Coast Railways. The main line of the latter passing through to Brighton, and the Tunbridge & Reading branches of the former being all connected. Previous to the traffic of these lines, the place consisted of a few houses forming a mere hamlet; but on the opening up of the railway, a transition took place and the village was turned into a busy thriving town, which has gradually developed to its present size, and continues yearly to increase.' (*Half-holiday Handbooks. Round Reigate*, 1881.) Draper and outfitter Nicol & Son occupies the prominent corner site, opposite the Market Hall, and next door is a branch of J. Sainsbury.

This block of Victorian Redhill remains unchanged apart, of course, from the shopfronts.

Market Hall, 1980. A sad day for Redhill, with the loss of its imposing principal structure.

Lloyds Bank building with its pretty little cupola reminds us that we are still in the same place; otherwise the fortress-like Warwick Quadrant totally dominates the scene.

Station Approach, 1978. Alongside the estate agents, on the left, is the car park for the Odeon cinema, and in the foreground is the cul-de-sac that is the station approach.

There is now a large roundabout where Station Road meets the newly constructed Princess Way. In 1997 the brewers Greene King built The Abbot, tacking it on to the end of the remaining portion of the Victorian shops in Station Road.

Ladbroke Road, 1981. The pub has already closed, awaiting the demolition crew and the new town centre development.

The southern end of Ladbroke Road has now disappeared, and access to the remaining portion is gained from the newly constructed Princess Way.

Ladbroke Road, 1981. This scene was viewed from the platform of Redhill station and is a sharp reminder of how much the town has changed in such a short space of time. In the centre, about to be demolished, stands The Locomotive pub; looming large over it is the ugly and, thankfully, short-lived *Surrey Mirror* building.

The scene is unrecognisable except for the spire of St Matthew's Church and the block of flats on the horizon. The Warwick Quadrant now dominates the area.

Ladbroke Road, 1975. Near the junction with Station Road and pictured here shortly before demolition, stood this row of old shops including the printing works for the old-established firm of S.C. Jennings. For a short period the old stables next door were used by the *Surrey Mirror* for their classified ads, blockmaking and photographic departments. When their old printing works opposite was demolished in the early 1970s those departments were accommodated in the concrete monstrosity that was built on the site.

The creation of the Warwick Quadrant and of Princess Way removed all trace of the southern end of Ladbroke Road.

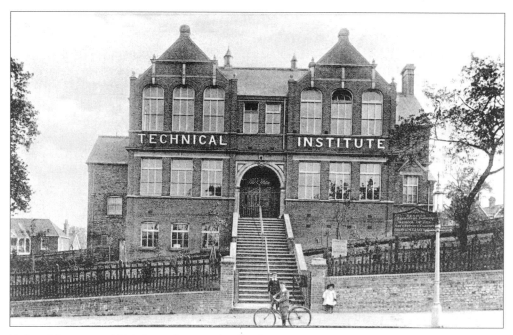

Technical Institute, *c.* 1906. Opened in 1895 by the Chairman of the Surrey County Council, this Institute was primarily used for evening classes, and as these grew in popularity so the Institute expanded. Extended variously over the years and using further accommodation over the shops in Station Road, the Institute had its death-knell finally sounded when the emphasis in further education was placed on full-time courses, and the County Council opened what is now East Surrey College in 1967.

The old Institute had outlived its usefulness and was demolished recently, to be replaced by houses.

Laker's Hotel, *c*. 1908. In 1858 the building was titled The Railway Hotel with Mr W. Wilkinson the licensee; however, by 1861 Richard and Muriel Laker, their six children and thirteen servants had taken up residence, and from that date the place was known as Laker's Hotel.

Station car-parking now occupies the plot of land in the foreground, but the hotel is very much as it was, externally.

Redstone Hill, *c.* 1906. The description of this area by R.F.D. Palgrave in his *Illustrated Handbook to Reigate* of 1860 holds much relevance today: 'The name of the hill arises from the bright tints of the sand strata of which it is formed. It commands sights of much beauty and interest, in the broad stretch of country sweeping up towards Tunbridge – in the thickset woods of Nutfield, upon the opposite hill – and in the view of the gorge below, which seems so narrow and inconsiderable, when contrasted with the mighty stream of continental traffic, that sets up and down it, night and day.'

Much of that 'mighty stream of continental traffic' used to travel along the A25 until the opening of the M25, which has relieved this road of its burden. The route down along Redstone Hollow and Hooley Lane has recently been laid with road humps to slow down and dissuade traffic from using the road as a cut-through avoiding Redhill centre. It seems to work.

Arthur Wood, pianoforte & music warehouse, Station Road, 1897. 'Established in 1868, Mr Wood was formerly principal tuner to the eminent pianoforte houses of Messrs. J. Brinsmead & Sons, with whom he also served his apprenticeship in the construction of pianos, so that he has had the benefit of a thorough practical training in every detail. The stock includes every variety and make, such as instruments by J. Broadwood & Sons, Collard & Collard, J. Brinsmead & Sons, Erard, Hopkinson, Allison, Ward etc. of the English makers; and those by Neumeyer, Ibach, Hermann, Schiedmayer, Bord etc. of the leading continental makers. American organs by Mason & Hamlin, Bell, Clough & Warren, Karn and others besides harmoniums, violins, guitars, banjos, autoharps etc. For the convenience of his customers he has adopted the hire-purchase system, by which arrangements can be made, and under easy circumstances, for purchasing instruments of all kinds.'

During the 1950s the shop was occupied by Carr-Woods, outfitter and tailor, and it is now an estate agent.

T. Padwick, pharmaceutical chemist, Station Road, 1897. 'Established in 1849, the premises consist of a double shop with large plate-glass windows and fittings in finest mahogany. Here will be found every description of surgical appliance, water and air cushions, invalid's conveniences, elastic stockings and water beds on sale or hire. English and foreign prescriptions are accurately dispensed in strict accordance with the pharmacopoeias of the respective countries, the best and purest chemicals only being used. Mr Padwick has attained an enviable reputation as an optician of no small repute, and is always prepared to supply spectacles, eye glasses, cameras, lenses, meteorological and mathematical instruments.'

The shop continued to be a chemist until fairly recently. In the 1950s it was J. Sampson's but now the site is split in two, one half being an estate agent and the other a sandwich shop.

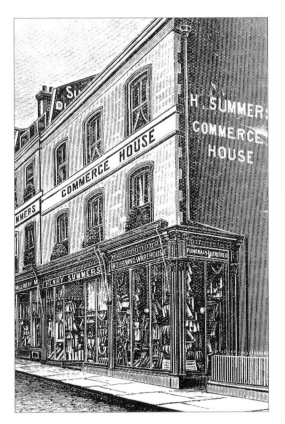

Henry Summers, draper, hosier and silk mercer, Station Road, 1897. 'The four plate-glass windows are dressed to the best advantage, and the assistants, under the direction of Mr Summers, make a tasteful display suggestive of the wealth of stock inside, whether silks, satins or plain or fancy dress materials, Mr Summers makes a special feature of dress materials, household linen etc. and here may be obtained all the celebrated makes, which are guaranteed to wear well. To maintain his high reputation, Mr Summers always keeps a large stock of hat and bonnet shapes of the latest and most approved fashion, ribbons, flowers, feathers, ornaments and every requisite.'

A dreary example of recent architecture has replaced the four plate-glass windows of Henry Summers' shopfront, which more recently became John Nicol Ltd.

St Matthew's Church and Schools, *c.* 1910. The church was consecrated by the Bishop of Winchester in 1866 with the National School for Boys being added in 1872 to accommodate 170 pupils. It was enlarged in 1881 and again in 1884 to include girls and infants.

The school has closed and is now offices, and St Matthew's Road now links up with Cromwell Road. Many of the substantial Victorian houses that formerly lined Station Road have gone, some being replaced by the large office block now occupied by Toyota (GB) Ltd.

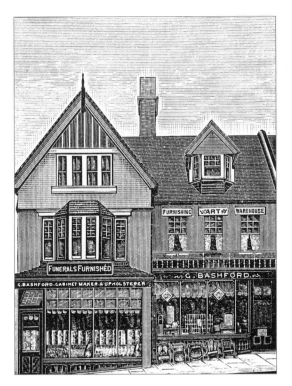

G. Bashford, cabinet maker and upholsterer. 'Here may be seen a splendid assortment of high-class goods, including a display of finely carved oak and mahogany side-boards, oak, walnut and mahogany drawing and dining-room suites, upholstered in appropriate materials, antique furniture, and a choice of art and valuable curios.

Mr. Bashford keeps a full staff of skilled and experienced workmen busy all year, and every inch of space is utilised for showrooms, warehouse and stores. All the cabinet making and upholstery work is guaranteed to be perfect and none but the best samples of carpets, floorcloths, hearthrugs, linoleums, cretonnes, blinding, bedsteads, bedding etc. is kept.

A special feature is made of the removal of furniture by road or rail by Pantechnicon vans, or it is warehoused in large dry rooms for the convenience of patrons.'

After many usages the building is now a bedroom and bathroom supplier.

Linkfield Corner, *c.* 1919. Just over Raffle's (Reffell's) Bridge is the parade of shops at Linkfield Corner built in the late nineteenth century. Wilfrid Hooper is scathing of the style of buildings being erected at this period. 'The early stages of this building activity, which included the erection of much of Redhill town, coincided unfortunately with one of the most debased periods of English architecture.'

An interesting chapter in the life of the area is recalled by Charles Preston, former editor of the *Surrey Mirror*: 'For 2 weeks, Billingsgate fish market set up at the old brewery buildings at Linkfield Corner. The fish merchants objected and the market returned to its home in Sept. 1939. Many hundreds of tons of fish were sold at Redhill to retailers, whose lorries were parked in long lines in Cromwell Road and the porters in white jackets and wearing their leather hats, on which they carried the boxes, turned the area into some resemblance to its real home.'

Shaw's Corner, *c.* 1905. The foundation stone for St Paul's Presbyterian Church was laid in 1901 and built to a design by George Lethbridge, architect. In front of the church stands a beautiful marble drinking fountain, erected to the memory of Edward Gedge, a Redhill resident who died while walking in the mountains in Zermatt, Switzerland in 1897 and whose tombstone is in the graveyard at St Peter's English Church in Zermatt. The cottage to the right was built in 1893.

St Paul's is now the United Reformed Church, and the drinking fountain now stands rather forlornly by the roadside at Whitepost Hill having made way for the war memorial in 1923. Being situated on an island in the middle of a busy road junction, it is unlikely that many people nowadays are aware of the inscription at its base: 'The bronze represents the triumphant struggle of mankind against the difficulties that beset him in the path of life. Shielding and bearing onward the child, the figure holds aloft the symbol of self-sacrifice to light the way. The flaming cross is used to indicate the suffering endured by men in the war. Flames consume the flesh. The spirit is unconquerable.' The sculptor was R.R. Goulden.

Batts Hill, *c.* 1910. At the bottom of the hill stands the lodge house to Linkfield House, a property dating from the early nineteenth century and part of the Monson estate. It had been let to private residents until the 1930s when it was purchased by the London County Council as a nursing home.

The lodge is a private residence now; Linkfield House is a Territorial Army Centre, having been purchased by TAVRA (South East) in the 1960s. With recent government cuts having been announced, the future of the centre is in doubt.

J. Worsfold, Alderney Diary. 'It says much for Mr. Worsfold that he is in a position to supply, twice daily, pure Alderney milk from the choice herd of cows of H.E. Gurney Esq., and fresh butter is made daily upon the premises. Families can be supplied with new-laid eggs and clotted cream fresh from Devonshire every day, and there is never any scarcity of dairy-fed pork and sausages in season.

In proof of the excellence of Mr. Worsfold's establishment, we would call attention to the fact that he has catered for the Cottage Hospital for 10 years, and further, that he supplies the medical gentlemen of the district with milk, and this should go far to command confidence in the purity and genuineness of the dairy produce supplied by him.'

Most of the eastern side of Brighton Road has been rebuilt.

T. Tupper, bicycle and tricycle manufacturer. 'Redhill is no exception to the rule which obtains in nearly every town in the kingdom in the shape of a manufactory for bicycles and tricycles. Mr. Tupper's establishment in Brighton Road is a prosperous and progressive concern, well known to Wheelmen. The proprietor claims that his "Paragon" cycles with cushion tyres are the best on the market, and, so far as local circles are concerned, the assertion has been put to the test and proved. Great rivalry has existed amongst wheelmen of the Wanderers Cycling Club (Redhill) as to the winning of the President's prize at the annual meeting, but all competitors have been out-distanced by the rider of a "Paragon" and the coveted distinction has been won on one of these machines for four years in succession. The "Paragon" is one of the neatest, most serviceable, swiftest and most satisfactory machines on the market, and includes every feature that has found favour in the cycling world.'

A newly constructed office block for Hall & Co. awaits new tenants.

Brighton Road, *c.* 1905. The railway bridge known as The Reading Arch was constructed to carry the line through to Reading in 1849. In 1901 it was widened and rebuilt along with the tunnel at the station and the road bridges over the Reading line. This work was carried out by the South Eastern Railway Company but the major portion of the cost was borne by the Borough Council. St Joseph's church can be seen just above the bridge, to the left.

The brick-built bridge has been replaced by one of girder construction and St Joseph's Roman Catholic church has been demolished in favour of an office block.

Grove Hill Road, *c*. 1908. This area was laid out in 1859, along with Bridge and Ridgeway Roads, on land sold by the London & Brighton Railway Company to the National Freehold Land Society.

Buckland's of Redhill, furnishers, began trading at this site around the turn of the century having been established by William Buckland at Cromwell Road. A small way up the hill and to the left runs Garlands Road which has been much altered in the last decade, with many Victorian houses being demolished and new apartment blocks built in their place.

London Road, *c.* 1914. Four public houses stood within yards of one another at the southern end of London Road: The Somers Arms (closed 1841), The Marquis of Granby, The Greyhound and The New Inn.

The New Inn closed in the 1990s and reopened as a plumbing and bathroom supplier in 1997. The horse trough formerly stood against the wall of The Firs, on the other side of Mill Street.

Hooley Lane, *c.* 1909. Before the railway was built, this was the main route up Redstone Hill. After Station Road was completed, however, it was decided that the road should extend up the hill, linking with Hooley Lane at the brow of the hill. Beyond the bridge is a gasometer belonging to the Redhill Gas Company, incorporated in 1865, which became The East Surrey Gas Company in 1921 when it absorbed the Reigate Gas Company.

The brick arch of the railway bridge has been replaced with one of metal girder construction, and the street is now one way only at this point. The row of Railway Cottages has been demolished.

Mill Street, *c.* 1905. A delivery van has pulled up outside Rose Brewery on this ancient roadway. To the left of the picture is The Firs, formerly a public house, The Somers Arms.

In the days before the railway this road provided the main east–west route from Reigate to Godstone and beyond; now it is a little-used access road for local motorists.

The view from Redhill Common, *c.* 1905. Mill Street, in the foreground, is regarded as being one of the oldest streets in the Borough, having been the main east–west road before the construction of the railways and the subsequent building of Station Road and its extension up to the summit of Redstone Hill. At this time Stansfield & Co. had their Rose Brewery at no. 3.

The changes in the tree-line and undergrowth make it difficult to pin-point radical changes.

No. 10 Hooley Lane. Hooley (Howleigh) manor was granted to Joseph Jekyll in 1697, along with the manor of Reygate, and was that area between Redhill and Earlswood, not the village we now know as Hooley, north of Merstham. When Reigate converted to Borough status in 1837, it comprised two wards with Hooley a part of the eastern ward. This house is believed to be one of the oldest surviving houses in Redhill, dating back to 1590. According to the Domestic Buildings Research Group (Surrey): 'The hearth facing only one way indicates a small house with the service room in the other bay. Few of these smaller houses have survived.'

The house was extensively renovated in 1984, retaining some of the original features, including part of the timber-framing and an inglenook hearth. The front door has been placed centrally and the end wall has been painted, but otherwise the house still looks charming. At some stage, probably in the 1930s, the house was used as a pub while The Marquis of Granby was being rebuilt on the adjacent site.

White Post Hill, *c.* 1900. This little group of houses nestling atop White Post Hill was built in the late 1700s and was once part of the all-encompassing Somers/Somerset estate. Miss Eleanor Isherwood, a resident there since 1930, remembers seeing a small black aeroplane approaching from the direction of the railway dropping its bombs as it drew near. 'The final bomb (of nine) fell in the front garden of Apsley in Upper Bridge Road, severely damaging the building but the residents escaped unhurt.' (Preston, *The Borough of Reigate in Wartime, 1939–1945.*)

The end house has been altered somewhat but those to the right remain very similar. The sandy wasteland of 1900 has been colonised by laurels, bracken and various trees, making this the only view that comes close to matching the original.

St John's Redhill. 'Perched upon a knoll of rising ground, midway down the hillside, is St John's, the Redhill District Church. It was built in 1843 (Mr Knowles, the architect) at a cost of about £5,000 and will hold nearly 700 people. The site of the church is more picturesque than desirable, for the narrow limits of the hillock prevent a much needed increase of accommodation.' Thus was the scene described in 1860 by R.F.D. Palgrave in his *Illustrated Handbook to Reigate*.

The small cottages in the foreground have been replaced by a block of town houses but the well-worn path remains the same as does the pub (on the right), albeit under a different name; The Elm Shades is now The Earlswood Arms.

Linkfield Lane, *c.* 1900. Thomas Phillips was a florist and gardener living at no. 8 at this time. This was one of the very last thatched cottages in Redhill; sadly, it was demolished in the 1970s to make way for modern housing.

No. 8 Linkfield Lane, 1998.

St Joseph's Convent, *c.* 1940. The Sisters of the Christian Retreat opened a convent at Gore House in Cavendish Road in 1887 and in the same year opened secondary and primary schools for 32 pupils. In 1889 they moved to Ladbroke Road; the chapel and assembly hall opened in 1923; and in 1937 a new school block was added. By 1955 there were 190 pupils on the school roll.

In 1976 a new primary school was built in Linkfield Lane and the secondary school amalgamated with St Bede's. The nuns left in 1990 and in 1991 the school and most of the convent buildings were sold for housing development. The former chapel has become part of the Parish Centre.

Earlswood Asylum, *c*. 1900. The foundation stone for this magnificent building was laid by Albert, the Prince Consort, in June 1853; he returned in July 1855 for the opening ceremony. The Prince and Princess of Wales laid a memorial stone for an extension in 1869 but despite this prominent royal patronage, R.F.D. Palgrave comments in 1860: 'The present number of inmates in the Idiot Asylum is 276. It is vexing to know, that there is ample supply of cases outside, and room for twice as many patients inside this building, if the Institution had sufficient funds for their support.' Robert Phillips describes the institution in 1885: 'The inmates, of whom there are about 600, are those whose deficiency of intellect is from birth, so differing from the forms of mental affliction known as lunacy, imbecility and madness. Some are private patients, having separate rooms and attendants, and paying accordingly, others are received on ordinary terms, and the remainder are elected (by the subscribers) for terms of years or for life.'

The avenue of magnificent conifers planted in the early part of this century makes this a difficult scene to match to the original photograph. Along with many similar former asylums, the Royal Earlswood is lying empty and forlorn awaiting redevelopment.

CHAPTER SEVEN

WATCH THESE SPACES

The photographs on the following pages were taken between September 1997 and May 1998 and depict those areas that are threatened with change. Some of these sites will already have been completed by the time this book is published while others will have to wait to learn their fate. One thing is certain, however; change will continue to take place.

Woodhatch Lodge, the former Crusader Insurance Co. building, is currently being developed by Canon UK.

Earlswood Common, Redhill. Next to Redhill Golf Club on the site of Hill End, 18 four- and five-bedroomed houses are being built.

Wiggie Lane, Redhill. The former Foxboro Yoxall site is currently being developed.

Frenches Road School, Redhill, its fate still undecided.

East Road, Reigate. The former South Eastern Gas Board site awaits a housing development.

North Street, Redhill. The Driving Test Centre awaits demolition.

Lesbourne Road, Reigate. The bus garage has been unused for some time and various options for re-use have been put forward.

Station Road, Redhill. Decorators' merchants C. Brewer & Sons Ltd moved to their new premises in Brighton Road at the end of 1997.

Castlefield Road, Reigate. Some 30,000 square feet of office space is currently under construction opposite the Town Hall.

Chapel Road, Redhill. Houses are about to be erected on this plot overlooking the 1890 Salvation Army hall.

The Town Hall, Castlefield Road, Reigate. Plans are afoot for centralisation of the council's offices which would mean rebuilding on this site.

The Royal Earlswood Hospital, Redhill. A wonderful set of buildings erected from 1855 onwards now await conversion.

St Matthew's Road, Redhill. The Royal British Legion Club has just been bulldozed.

Prices Lane, Woodhatch. The office block has been knocked down and housing is being built in its place.

London Road, Reigate. The railway station and former goods yard are at long last being rebuilt.

Castlefield Road, Reigate. Redland plc have left their old headquarters building and it is awaiting a new tenant or redevelopment.

High Street, Redhill. This block of 1960s shops and offices awaits change.

Bibliography

Dines and Edmunds, *The Geology of the County around Reigate & Dorking* (1933, HMSO)

Farries, K.G. and Mason, M.T., *The Windmills of Surrey and Inner London* (1966, Charles Skilton Ltd)

Half-holiday Handbooks. Round Reigate (1881 Marshall, Japp & Co.)

Harcourt-Burrage, E., *Reigate Home & Foreign, Past and Present* (1901)

Hooper, Dr W., *Reigate. Its Story through the Ages* (1945)

Ingram, A. and Pendrill, M., *Memoirs of Yesterday* (1984)

——, *Reflections of Yesterday* (1982)

——, *Social Scenes of Yesterday* (1992)

Illustrated Business Guide to Reigate, Redhill and Horley (1892, Walser & Grist, Hove)

Kelly's Directories from 1891

Ogilvy, J.S., *A Pilgrimage in Surrey* (1914)

Palgrave, R.F.D., *Illustrated Handbook to Reigate* (1860)

Phillips, R., *A Geographical, Historical and Topographical Description of the Borough of Reigate and Surrounding Districts* (1885)

Preston, C., *The Borough of Reigate in Wartime 1939–1945*

Surrey Archaeological Society (reprinted by Kohler & Coombes, 1979)

Wilcox, J., *Memories of South Park* (1996)

Technical Information

All of the modern photographs were taken on Nikon FA and FM2 cameras with 50mm and 28mm lenses using Ilford FP4, Delta 100 and 400 film processed in ID 11. The prints were made on Ilford Multigrade paper using a Leitz Focomat and hand-processed.

For advice on the availability of reprints of the photographs appearing in this book contact the author at 'Goodness Gracious', Jayes Park Courtyard, Lake Road, Ockley, Surrey, RH5 5RR. Telephone 01306 621474.

Acknowledgements

To all those people that I have spoken to in my search for information and enlightenment, I offer my grateful thanks for their help. I am particularly indebted to Chris Hoskins, Sean Hawkins and the Local Studies Library, Guildford, for allowing me to copy photographs and postcards from their collections. I have striven to check all the facts that are printed here but, inevitably, with any work that relies upon written and verbal testimonies, errors will be found. Forgive me if what you read is not how you would have it.

BRITAIN IN OLD PHOTOGRAPHS

ton
hersham
hbourne

ound Bakewell
ham & Tooting
rnes, Mortlake & Sheen
rnet & the Hadleys
rnet Past & Present
th
aconsfield
dfordshire at War
dworth
fast
erley
kley
deford
ston
hop's Stortford &
awbridgeworth
hopstone & Seaford II
ckburn
tchley
xwich
aintree & Bocking at Work
entwood
dgwater & the River
arrett
dlington
istol
ixton & Norwood
ckingham & District
ry
shbury

mberwell, Peckham &
Dulwich
mbridge
nnock Yesterday & Today
nterbury Cathedral
nterbury Revisited
rdigan & the Lower Teifi
Valley
ound Carlisle
stle Combe to Malmesbury

Chadwell Heath
Cheadle
Chelmsford
Cheltenham in the 1950s
Cheltenham Races
Chesham Yesterday & Today
Around Chichester
Chiswick & Brentford
Chorley & District
Around Cirencester
Clacton-on-Sea
Around Clitheroe
Colchester 1940–70
Coventry at War
Cowes & East Cowes
Around Crawley
Cromer
Croydon
Crystal Palace, Penge &
Anerley

Darlington at Work & Play
Darlington II
Dawlish & Teignmouth
Around Devizes
East Devon at War
Dorchester
Dorking Revisited
Dumfries
Dundee at Work
Durham: Cathedral City
Durham People
Durham at Work

Ealing, Hanwell, Perivale &
Greenford
Ealing & Northfields
The Changing East End
Around East Grinstead
East Ham
Around Eastbourne
Elgin
Eltham
Ely
Enfield

Esher
Exmouth & Budleigh Salterton
Farnborough II
Fleetwood
Folkestone II
Folkestone III
The Forest of Dean Revisited
Frome
Fulham

Galashiels
Around Gillingham
Gloucestershire at Work
North Gloucestershire at
War
South Gloucestershire at War
Goudhurst to Tenterden
Grantham
Great Yarmouth II
Greenwich
Greenwich & Woolwich

Hackney II
Hackney, Homerton & Dalston
From Haldon to Mid-
Dartmoor
Hammersmith & Shepherd's
Bush
Hampstead to Primrose Hill
Around Harrogate
Harrow & Pinner
Hastings & St Leonards
Hayes & West Drayton
Around Haywards Heath
Around Helston
Around Henley-on-Thames
Herefordshire
Around Highworth
Hitchin
Holderness
Hong Kong
Huddersfield II
Huddersfield III

Ilford to Hainault
Ilfracombe
Ipswich Revisited

Islington
Jersey III

Kendal Revisited
Kensington & Chelsea
East Kent at War
Keswick & the Central Lakes
Kingston
Kirkby & District
Kirkby & District II
Kirkby Lonsdale
Knowle & Dorridge

The Lake Counties at Work
Lambeth, Kennington &
Clapham
Lancashire
The Lancashire Coast
Lancashire Railways
East Lancashire at War
Lancing & Sompting
Leeds in the News
Around Leek
East of Leicester
Leicester at Work
Leicestershire People
Letchworth
Lewisham & Deptford III
Lincoln
Lincoln Cathedral
The Lincolnshire Coast
The Lincolnshire Wolds
Liverpool
Llandudno
Around Lochaber
Theatrical London
Loughborough
Lowestoft
Luton
Lye & Wollescote
Lympne Airfield
Lytham St Annes

Around Maidenhead
Manchester
Manchester Road & Rail
Mansfield

SUTTON'S PHOTOGRAPHIC HISTORY OF TRANSPORT

To order any of these titles please telephone our distributor, Littlehampton Book Services on 01903 828800
For a catalogue of these and our other titles please ring Emma Leitch on 01453 731114